WORSHIPFUL
COMPANY OF
FLETCHERS

WORSHIPFUL COMPANY OF FLETCHERS

POEMS

JAMES TATE

THE ECCO PRESS

Copyright © 1994 by James Tate

THE ECCO PRESS
100 West Broad Street
Hopewell, New Jersey 08525
Published simultaneously in Canada by
Penguin Books Canada Ltd., Ontario
Printed in the United States of America

Designed by Vincent J. Janoski

Library of Congress Cataloging-in-Publication Data

Tate, James, 1943-
Worshipful Company of Fletchers : poems / James Tate. — 1st ed.
p.   cm.
I. Title.
PS3570.A8W67   1994
811'.54—dc20   94-9821
ISBN 0-88001-380-x

The text of this book is set in Horley Old Style

For Dara

Grateful acknowledgment is made to the editors of the following magazines in which these poems first appeared: *The New Yorker, American Poetry Review, Antaeus, Colorado Review, Cut Bank, Field, Gettysburg Review, Harvard Review, Iowa Review, The Missouri Review, The Nation, New England Quarterly, The New York Times, Painted Bride Quarterly,* and *Ploughshares.*

Contents

I always ran Home to Awe when a child, if anything befell me.
He was an awful Mother, but I liked him better than none.

—Emily Dickinson

WORSHIPFUL
COMPANY OF
FLETCHERS

GO, YOUTH

I was in a dreamstate and this was causing a problem
with the traffic. I felt lonely, like I'd missed the boat,
or I'd found the boat and it was deserted. In the middle
of the road a child's shoe glistened. I walked around it.
It woke me up a little. The child had disappeared. Some
mysteries are better left alone. Others are dreary, distasteful,
and can disarrange a shadow into a thing of unspeakable beauty.
Whose child is that?

WHAT A PATIENT DOES

I follow the tinkle of the lead llama's bell,
a shadow in the memory of man, while maintaining
a strict radio silence. I could see a Chieftain
on a hill surveying ancient ruins.
The breath of leaves and moss and green daylight,
a stray pig snapping at his ankles.
From the tar-pit of the obvious I did nothing.
I maintained a strict radio silence, humming.
Flocks of beetles settled on the leaves of tangerine trees.
A tiny ladybird beetle dreamed I was its loyal ally.
To my right is a man reading on a rock.
He thinks he has renounced the world, but there he is,
occupying a little space. An empty chair beside him
has another idea. It is rocking to and fro'.
I tell myself: I'll move like water over this undergrowth.
And then I draw back and hold my breath. Something
I've never seen before: a pig breaking in two.
Fingers of lightning flash. The llama looks
very much like a sheep with a long neck. Its head
is a cloud of dust and gas located among the stars.

AUTOSUGGESTION:
USS NORTH CAROLINA

And that is the largest battleship in the world, I said.
And see how small it really is. Isn't that encouraging?
She pointed her head toward the drinking fountain,
but was having none of it. A dog from the mental ward
hopped over her. We had driven all the way to Surf City
for some peace and, it's not as though it eluded us
so much as it did circle us. The pelicans were on display.
They did pelican-like dives into the surf and came up
wanting bit parts in a movie other than ours.
We were surprisingly graceful and called Pest Control.
That whole day was like a dream leaking into our satchel.
It was stained permanently, but so attractive
we couldn't have designed it better, and we knew nothing
about design. The battleship seemed stalled forever,
or it was a little intimidated by its own reputation.
Whatever the case, we held the idea of a torpedo
gingerly in our minds and meandered without launching it.
Most of the natives were under house arrest.
They wore ankle bracelets and watched us from their windows
or monitors. We couldn't go any farther than this.
We were touring our Armed Forces here and there.
Some of the ammo felt moldy. The Officers, though,
were made of steel, soft and pliable,
like stuffed animals. They wet their beds—that seemed

to be the unifying principle. But what did we know?
We were rank amateurs. We were poseurs of the worst sort.
We were out of our league. We belonged in little league
uniforms, but we couldn't afford them, and our sponsors
were idiots and dunces and drifters and no-count
amalgamated mud merchants. This left us free of debt
and free of riches, which can be so heavy to transport.
We were airy and free and broke and lost
figure skaters or trigger fish, whatever.
And whenever one of the ships felt like sinking
we just picked up magazines and pretended to read
about something else, like a migraine headache
discovered still pounding inside a 10,000-year-old
snowman holding up the North Pole. Incredible! we'd say.
And, who could believe in that? 35,000 tons of history,
going, going—so long. Next, we are going to visit
planets of the solar system, like Burma and Senegal.
But the Department of Housing and Urban Development
says there is heartache and neuralgia starting to blossom there,
but also hydroponics is being discovered.
We have decided to travel by hydroplane,
though, sadly, there is no water anywhere as yet.

A MISSED OPPORTUNITY

A word sits on the kitchen counter
next to the pitcher of cream
with its blue cornflowers bent.
Perhaps a guest left it in a hurry
or as a tip for good service,
or as a fist against some imagined
insult. Or it fell with some old
plaster from the ceiling, a word
some antediluvian helpmate
hushed up. It picked itself up
from the floor, brushed itself off
and, somehow, scratched its way
up the cupboards. It appears to be
a word of considerable strength
and even significance, but I can't
bring myself to look into its gaze.
The cornflowers are pointing toward
the cookies not far away. An expert
could be called to defuse the word,
but it is Sunday and they are still
sleeping or singing, and, besides that,
the word seems to have moved again
on its own, and now it appears warm
and welcoming, it throbs with life
and a sincere desire to understand me.
It looks slightly puzzled and hurt,
as though I. . . . I take a step toward it,
I hold out my hand. "Friend," I say,

but it is shrinking, it is going away
to its old home in the familiar
cold dark of the human parking lot.

50 VIEWS OF TOKYO

Only fly-specks remain.
I have not a thought in my head.
My head is a giant pumpkin with a thousand legs.
That must be the elusive thought I was after.
I am feeling a degree of relief and even confidence
after that exercise. Now I remember December 22, 1935.
A bunch of young officers, including yours truly,
met in a restaurant in Shinjuku to discuss a plot.
That's all I remember. The communal spirit
of the valley drifted away. Maybe it was sad.
Then again it might have been a great joke.
I was going to publish *A Secret History*,
but I lost it or it got stolen, perhaps in a subway.
These days I relish a second opinion.
Could there have been another, a better war?
I think I was the one who ran away, who climbed a tree
and then another tree, and then the last one.
I was suffering from postnatal insanity.
I ran into the Matuya Department Store and said
to the pretty young salesgirl, "Your papa and I
thank you from the bottom of our hearts!"
She started to giggle, and then a few tears eked out
and I sat down on the floor exhausted.
It felt like 1945, like everything was finished.
I remember at some point I had leeches on my face.
An American soldier offered to remove them.
I thought, it's too soon to harvest them,

they'll get much bigger. The Hotel Kaijo was occupied.
I was wishing I could sit on top
of The Five Stories pagoda in Ueno Park
as in the first days when I had no thoughts.
Once I sat on the toilet in the lobby
of the wrestling amphitheater for several hours
astonished that this was my life, my only life,
and I had nothing better to do than sit there.
I didn't care even a little bit about wrestling
and I thought that made me some kind of freakish monster.
If someone had walked in on me and said, "Excuse me,
but would you like to join me for some Wakame seaweed from
        Naruto
cooked with new bamboo shoots and leaf buds?
Perhaps we can solve a few of those riddles
so troubling to young persons like yourself,"
I might have bitten his nose. I was a wild animal
without a soul or a home or a name.
And now I see it wasn't a stage I was going through.
That stage, that stageless stage, was my home
and my name and my soul, and the maze of years
and the endless palaver, the well-wishing
like a blue smoke circling, the world-order
tilting this way and that, the extinct species
coming back to haunt, the rice birds and the butterflies
circling and disappearing, O I longed for one firm
handshake and a kick in the butt I could understand.
A terribly pretty snake stared into my one good eye

and I said this is something I can understand.
After a while I hung it from my neck
and went waltzing with the devil on Asakusa Show Street.
That's when we dreamed up the war to kill
this boredom and its hallowed tradition of proscribed behavior.
Soon everyone would be hanging themselves from the gaslights
and cackling with otherworldly delight.
A child played a lute with such purity of sound
streetcars stopped to applaud.
And a horse made a speech praising the damned.
These are my memories, a white Navy Hospital,
a kiss outside the British Embassy.

WHAT THE CITY WAS LIKE

The city was full of blue devils,
and, once, during an eclipse, the river
began to glow, and a small body walked out of it
carrying a wooden ship full of vegetables
which we mistook for pearls.
We made necklaces of them, and tiaras and bracelets,
and the small body laughed until
its head fell off, and soon enough we realized
our mistake, and grew weak with our knowledge.
Across town, a man lived his entire life
without ever going out on the street.
He destroyed his part of the city many times
without getting off his sofa.
But that neighborhood has always blossomed afresh.
Pixies germinated in the still pools under streetlights.
Cattle grazed in back of the bakery
and helped deliver baked goods to the needy.
A mouse issued commands in a benevolent, judicious, and cheerful
        manner.
A small, headless body lay in the road,
and passersby clicked their heels.
Across the street the Military Academy
had many historic spots on its windows,
thanks, in part, to the rivers and canals
which carried large quantities of freight
into the treasure house of maps
and music scores necessary for each war.
The spots were all given names by the janitors—

River of Unwavering Desire, River of Untruth,
Spring of Spies, Rill of Good Enough Hotelkeepers,
and then, of course, there was the Spot of Spots.
Nobody paid any attention to the wars,
though there must have been a few or more.
The citizens of the city were wanderers
who did not live in any one place
but roamed the boulevards and alleyways
picking up gumwrappers and setting them down again.
We were relieved when modern ice skating
was finally invented: the nuns glided in circles
for days on end, and this was the greatest blessing.
Behind City Hall salt was mined
under a powerful magnifying glass,
and each grain was tasted by someone
named Mildred until she became a stenographer
and moved away, and no one could read
her diacritical remarks, except the little devils.
For years Mildred sent cards at Christmas,
and then nothing, and no one said a thing.
The city was covered with mountains
which ran straight down the center,
and on the southern tip there were several
volcanoes which could erupt on demand.
Or so it was said, though no one demanded proof.
It was a sketchy little volcano of normal girth
where Dolley Madison hosted her parties

more often that I care to remember.
She served ice cream when she was coming.
She came early and stayed late, as they say,
until all the lights were off and the guests
had lost all hope of regaining their senses.
It is not certain if she possessed a cupcake at that time.
She might have had one in her cellar
as no one was allowed to penetrate her there.
And then the prairie dogs arrived
and caused incorrect pips to appear
on the radar screen, for which they became famous,
and which precipitated the rapid decline
of the Know Nothings—not a minute too soon.
In the days that followed children were always screaming.
You could set their hair on fire and, sure enough,
they'd start screaming.

THE GREAT ROOT SYSTEM

When the birds talk, I answer.
When they are hungry, I need feed.
They desire to propagate, I do too.
But the story ends here, it goes
nowhere. It's just too early
in the morning to think anything through.
A thought starts up, it's like tickling
in my brain. My motor's running
but I'm almost out of gas.
I look at my appointment calendar—
spider webs and chicken scratches.
Ah, I see, there's a ladybug coming tomorrow.
For a block of wood, I am so very busy.
I am waiting for the phone to ring.
Is that you, Tweetie? Not a peep.
I flick on the television: no news
is still no news. It's *terribly* early.
It's not as though I have a cow to milk,
or do I? A lovely bovine ruminant
would provide such satisfaction
at this moment. Or a cowbird—
amazing to think of the cowbird
because it makes no nest, and lays
its eggs in the nests of other birds.
What a concept! And, usually, the foster parents—
listen to me! I'm talking of birds
as foster parents, this is really fun—
do not seem to notice anything strange

about the young cowbird, which may be
twice the size of their own chicks.
(This thought has completely exhausted me,
I'm seriously considering a return
to the dark—but safe—underbelly of sleep.)
My own humanity has overwhelmed me,
it has nearly defeated me, the me who was
trying to rise up. It—that is, my own
humanity—seethed up when I least wanted it.
Following the magnetic forces of other worlds,
the birds fly in all directions,
less bird-like than myself.

LOYALTY

This is the hardest part:
when I came back to life
I was a good family dog
and not too friendly to strangers.
I got a thirty-five dollar raise
in salary, and through the pea-soup fogs
I drove the General, and introduced him
at rallies. I had a totalitarian approach
and was a massive boost to his popularity.
I did my best to reduce the number of people.
The local bourgeoisie did not exist.
One of them was a mystic
and walked right over me
as if I were a bed of hot coals.
This is par for the course—
I will be employing sundry golf metaphors
henceforth, because a dog, best friend
and chief advisor to the General, should.
While dining with the General I said,
"Let's play the back nine in a sacred rage.
Let's tee-off over the foredoomed community
and putt ourselves thunderously, touching bottom."
He drank it all in, rugged and dusky.
I think I know what he was thinking.
He held his automatic to my little head
and recited a poem about my many weaknesses,
for which I loved him so.

LITTLE POEM WITH
ARGYLE SOCKS

Behind every great man
there sits a rat.
And behind every great rat,
there's a flea.
Beside the flea there is an encyclopedia.
Every now and then the flea sneezes, looks up,
and flies into action, reorganizing history.
The rat says, "God, I *hate* irony."
To which the great man replies,
"Now now now, darling, drink your tea."

A MANUAL OF ENLARGEMENT

Early on
I did some hopeful scratching
in my garden patch.
I saw green!
It's really nice this time.
It's beginning to seem like
a plausible life.
It's President's Day
and no one can find the President.
Also, there's a milkman
who refuses to deliver.
Oh well, I say, still I've got thirteen
dachshunds, and the woman sleeping on the train
fell off but wasn't hurt
as much as she was just plain surprised.
It's time to go to sleep,
but no one does, everyone's afraid
of falling off.
The World Series was a bust.
And last Christmas
everyone got what they deserved.
I don't mean that sarcastically.
This morning someone threw me a pancake
through their sunroof.
It was just what I needed
when I needed it most.
There's a pet squirrel
watching all of this,

I know that. That pleases me.
Perhaps I'm too easily pleased.
Fritz is the name I gave
to all of my dachshunds.
It seems to please them.
They are benign, all in a pile.
But they refuse to eat, nonetheless.
The guard dog fell to pieces.
Butterflies covered everything,
like a marmalade
that couldn't be staunched.
The heavens opened, the heavens closed.
The weather was inventing a new way
of expressing itself.
This was fine by me, a fine contribution.
There was a tunnel at the end of the fog.
What little meditation I had
was gone in a puff.
It was part of our plans, our city plans,
our even bigger plans, that we should circle
and take short cuts and maybe even fly over
all those obstacles
that were hitherto our lives.
This was good. We had a big,
unclear sense of this,
and that was exactly what we needed.
Semisacred bedtime stories,
Squirt bottles on the windowsill.

We had had enough of picnicking.
One of the court painters
also fell over, and then left
in spectacular disorder.
I opened a resort, a last resort,
and people milled around.
Then the buildings began to arrive
and it was politics as usual
until the woman of my dreams appeared
and it was a day at the races,
not tired, not too sad.
Frank and Lloyd and Betty said
nothing could have improved upon it,
and that was good enough for me.

HEAD OF A WHITE
WOMAN WINKING

She has one good bumblebee
which she leads about town
on a leash of clover.
It's as big as a Saint Bernard
but also extremely fragile.
People want to pet its long, shaggy coat.
These would be mostly whirling dervishes
out shopping for accessories.
When Lily winks they understand everything,
right down to the particle
of a butterfly's wing lodged
in her last good eye,
so the situation is avoided,
the potential for a cataclysm
is narrowly averted,
and the bumblebee lugs
its little bundle of shaved nerves
forward, on a mission
from some sick, young godhead.

LIKE A SCARF

The directions to the lunatic asylum were confusing;
most likely they were the random associations
and confused ramblings of a lunatic.
We arrived three hours late for lunch
and the lunatics were stacked up on their shelves,
quite neatly, I might add, giving credit where credit is due.
The orderlies were clearly very orderly, and they
should receive all the credit that is their due.
When I asked one of the doctors for a corkscrew
he produced one without a moment's hesitation.
And it was a corkscrew of the finest craftsmanship,
very shiny and bright not unlike the doctor himself.
"We'll be conducting our picnic under the great oak
beginning in just a few minutes, and if you'd care
to join us we'd be most honored. However, I understand
you have your obligations and responsibilities,
and if you would prefer to simply visit with us
from time to time, between patients, our invitation
is nothing if not flexible. And, we shan't be the least slighted
or offended in any way if, due to your heavy load,
we are altogether deprived of the pleasure
of exchanging a few anecdotes, regarding the mentally ill,
depraved, diseased, the purely knavish, you in your bughouse,
if you'll pardon my vernacular, O yes, and we in our crackbrain
daily rounds, there are so many gone potty everywhere we roam,
not to mention in one's own home, dead moonstruck.
Well, well, indeed we would have many notes to compare

if you could find the time to join us after your injections."
My invitation was spoken in the evenest tones,
but midway through it I began to suspect I was addressing
an imposter. I returned the corkscrew in a nonthreatening manner.
What, for instance, I asked myself, would a doctor, a doctor of the
    mind,
be doing with a corkscrew in his pocket?
This was a very sick man, one might even say dangerous.
I began moving away cautiously, never taking my eyes off of him.
His right eyelid was twitching guiltily, or at least anxiously,
and his smock flapping slightly in the wind.
Several members of our party were mingling with the nurses
down by the duck pond, and my grip on the situation
was loosening, the planks in my picnic platform were rotting.
I was thinking about the potato salad in an unstable environment.
A weeping spell was about to overtake me.
I was very close to howling and gnashing the gladiola.
I noticed the great calm of the clouds overhead.
And below, several nurses appeared to me in need of nursing.
The psychopaths were stirring from their naps,
I should say, their postprandial slumbers.
They were lumbering through the pines like inordinately sad
    moose.
Who could eat liverwurst at a time like this?
But, then again, what's a picnic without pathos?
Lacking a way home, I adjusted the flap in my head and
    duck-walked

down to the pond and into the pond and began gliding
around in circles, quacking, quacking like a scarf.
Inside the belly of that image I began
recycling like a sorry whim, sincerest regrets
are always best.

MORE LATER, LESS THE SAME

The common is unusually calm—they captured the storm
last night, it's sleeping in the stockade, relieved
of its duty, pacified, tamed, a pussycat.
But not before it tied the flagpole in knots,
and not before it alarmed the firemen out of their pants.
Now it's really calm, almost too calm, as though
anything could happen, and it would be a first.
It could be the worst thing that ever happened.
All the little rodents are sitting up and counting
their nuts. What if nothing ever happened again?
Would there be enough to "eke out an existence,"
as they say? I wish "they" were here now, kicking
up a little dust, mussing my hair, taunting me
with weird syllogisms. Instead, these are the windless,
halcyon days. The lull dispassion is upon us.
Serenity has triumphed in its mindless, atrophied way.
A school of Stoics walks by, eager, in its phlegmatic way,
to observe human degradation, lust and debauchery
at close quarters. They are disappointed,
but it barely shows on their faces. They are late Stoa,
very late. They missed the bus. They should have
been here last night. The joint was jumping.
But people change, they grow up, they fly around.
It's the same old story, but I don't remember it.
It's a tale of gore and glory, but we had to leave.
It could have turned out differently, and it did.
I feel much the same way about the city of Pompeii.
A police officer with a poodle cut squirts his gun

at me for saying that, and it's still just barely
possible that I didn't, and the clock is running
out on his sort of behavior. I'm napping in a wigwam
as I write this, near Amity Street, which is buried
under fifteen feet of ashes and cinders and rocks.
Moss and a certain herblike creature are beginning to
whisper nearby. I am beside myself, peering down,
senselessly, since, for us, in space, there is
neither above nor below; and thus the expression
"He is being nibbled to death by ducks" shines
with such style, such poise, and reserve,
a beautiful, puissant form and a lucid thought.
To which I reply "It is time we had our teeth examined
by a dentist." So said James the Lesser to James the More.

HOW THE POPE IS CHOSEN

Any poodle under ten inches high is a toy.
Almost always a toy is an imitation
of something grown-ups use.
Popes with unclipped hair are called *corded popes.*
If a Pope's hair is allowed to grow unchecked,
it becomes extremely long and twists
into long strands that look like ropes.
When it is shorter it is tightly curled.
Popes are very intelligent.
There are three different sizes.
The largest are called standard Popes.
The medium-sized ones are called miniature Popes.
I could go on like this, I could say:
"He is a squarely built Pope, neat,
well-proportioned, with an alert stance
and an expression of bright curiosity,"
but I won't. After a poodle dies
all the cardinals flock to the nearest 7-Eleven.
They drink Slurpies until one of them throws up
and then he's the new Pope.
He is then fully armed and rides through the wilderness alone,
day and night in all kinds of weather.
The new Pope chooses the name he will use as Pope,
like "Wild Bill" or "Buffalo Bill."
He wears red shoes with a cross embroidered on the front.
Most Popes are called "Babe" because
growing up to become a Pope is a lot of fun.
All the time their bodies are becoming bigger and stranger,

but sometimes things happen to make them unhappy.
They have to go to the bathroom by themselves,
and they spend almost all of their time sleeping.
Parents seem to be incapable of helping their little popes grow up.
Fathers tell them over and over again not to lean out of windows,
but the sky is full of them.
It looks as if they are just taking it easy,
but they are learning something else.
What, we don't know, because we are not like them.
We can't even dress like them.
We are like red bugs or mites compared to them.
We think we are having a good time cutting cartoons out of the
        paper,
but really we are eating crumbs out of their hands.
We are tiny germs that cannot be seen under microscopes.
When a Pope is ready to come into the world,
we try to sing a song, but the words do not fit the music too well.
Some of the full-bodied popes are a million times bigger than us.
They open their mouths at regular intervals.
They are continually grinding up pieces of the cross
and spitting them out. Black flies cling to their lips.
Once they are elected they are given a bowl of cream
and a puppy clip. Eyebrows are a protection
when the Pope must plunge through dense underbrush

in search of a sheep.

BECOMING A SCOUT

Alone in my tree house
I can hear snakes thinking—
they want eggs for breakfast,
eggs for lunch and dinner,
all the while under a cloud of frangipani perfume.
This is the snake's dream,
and listening to sitar music.
If I say they are "sloe-eyed,"
I won't know what I mean. Bottle-green,
moiling, with rapier wit,
sending radiograms
to the marcelled, saw-toothed boy named Tony
who is about to major in Natural History somewhere.
I don't know where, exactly.
He opposes progress, though some seems evident,
at least from up here.
I hope you don't think I am being namby-pamby
when I say frog spittle is upon me.
I belong to several City Garden Clubs
and I know what I mean.
I know the right way and the wrong way
of bracing a crotch in a tree.
Also, a hundred pounds of tree food
is worth more than a hundred hours of cavity work.
There are a lot of frauds in the tree surgery racket.
Well, I digress. What got me off?
Tony, the maladjusted Naturalist.
There are several things necessary

to understanding the snake mentality:
they have air pumps in the oral cavity region.
That's all. Well, I could add
that the thermoscopic eyes of the squid
perceive the heat-generating object
through photochemical reactions,
which is completely different—I mean,
this is so unsnakelike as to be irrelevant.
Let's pretend I never mentioned this last bit.
My mind is drifting, as if on a leaf, on a wave,
a warm current is pulling my brains out, away, away from me.
Therefore I must proceed in a thoughtless, indeed brainless,
fashion, which could prove painful,
though I shall barely notice.
My best friend is a black squirrel
and he is too busy to visit me just now.
His name is Fester N. Wildly.
I don't know what the N stands for.
Perhaps Norman. Or Nothing.
He has been married for five years
and is an automotive parts salesman.
What else do I know about Fester, my dear, dear friend?
Oh yes, he has fourteen children,
three of whom still live at home.
His wife's name is Arlene
and she is originally from Cincinnati.
In the evenings they like to play bridge.
They have a statue of me on their mantle.
They have me over to dinner on a regular basis,

like once a year, maybe. She calls me Perkwu,
though that is not even close to my real name.
My name is Spoimo, which I find strange.

ANNUAL REPORT

Only one Disorderly Person was reported
(No one cared enough to report me.).
Likewise, only one Noise Complaint
(Can the whole village be deaf?).
And, in an entire year, there was only one
case of Indecent Exposure
(Is no one paying attention?).
Talk about breaking records, in all of 1989
there was only one Disturbed Person
(I hope they spelled my name right.).
On the bright side, eleven persons
were reported missing, and thirty-six
were identified as Suspicious.
Three motor vehicles were abandoned.
And there were five Deer Complaints
(Well pardon us for existing.).

BACK TO NATURE

You should drive a big red convertible as fast as you can
into the heart of the forest, drink champagne, and say
witty things to all the creatures you meet.

Walk around kicking your tires, and if you meet any
of those endangered Camp Fire Girls, say *Wohelo!*

Don't you wish you had remembered to pack the pemmican!

If you pull out a white handkerchief you will almost certainly
be mistaken for a deer and shot.

Don't forget to put the top up if it rains.

When you are lost stay where you are.

Sleep is an excellent method for tracking down the jewel thieves.

When you roll over never let your body touch the ground.

THE WRONG WAY HOME

All night a door floated down the river.
It tried to remember little incidents of pleasure
from its former life, like the time the lovers
leaned against it kissing for hours
and whispering those famous words.
Later, there were harsh words and a shoe
was thrown and the door was slammed.
Comings and goings by the thousands,
the early mornings and late nights, years, years.
O they've got big plans, they'll make a bundle.
The door was an island that swayed in its sleep.
the moon turned the doorknob just slightly,
burned its fingers and ran,
and still the door said nothing and slept.
At least that's what they like to say,
the little fishes and so on.
Far away, a bell rang, and then a shot was fired.

THE NITROGEN CYCLE

Before the break-up of my country
I was content to lie under the kitchen sink
and gnaw on busted pipes.
There was a nest of mice
with whom I could exchange recipes.
When the military planes flew
too low over my house
I would stagger out into the yard
and sprinkle Tabasco sauce
on their dreamy vapor trails.
My head was full of larks
lost in a sing-along.

A Snake person walked out of the forest
and just stared at me.
"O Snake man," I said,
"have you seen my little brother?"

"My name," he finally replied,
"is Mr. Ashby. Please address me
by that name or I will embarrass you
by telling you a beautiful story."

"You'll always be Snake man to me,
inclined though you may be
to tell beautiful stories
behind the guise of a pseudonym,

because that's your nature.
You are a wily apparition, no doubt,
conjured by my own crumbling defenses."

Mr. Ashby cleared his throat and smiled:
"Baby's tears began to flow
from baby's blue eyes.
The baby's slippers
were starting to walk on their own.
It was a false baby
with false baby's breath. . . . "

"That would be my brother," I sighed.
"O thank you, thank you, thank you."

THE EARLY YEARS

Minnesota is the Gopher State.
Why? I don't know.
In Baseball, a homerun
is sometimes referred to
as a gopher ball. I know
nothing about this so-called
baseball. Huckleberries
are also known as gopherberries.
Bull snakes are likewise
alluded to as gopher snakes;
presumably, they hunt
and eat the little varmints.
There is a gopher
known as the pocket gopher.
He would probably fit
in a pocket quite snugly.
I think gopher wood
is yellow of hue.
In southern Florida
there is a tree
with snowy, white flowers.
It has a hard, yellow wood
and yields a yellow dye.
Now if this is the wood
you are suggesting, please
tell me how I can get
to southern Florida
in time. I know this means

little to you, but I am over
six hundred years old.

*

I hated the idea of leaving
everyone behind. They were
a violent bunch, but who isn't?
Somehow we did it, I stopped
asking why. We snatched some birds,
roped a couple of giraffes, etc.
What a leave-taking, knowing
it will never be the same,
but it will be just the same,
as if to say, "I love swimming,
but I hate water." I might also
add that I packed poorly.

*

Although my sons were only
a hundred years old, they
were beginning to walk funny
and talk in riddles and pinch
one another's wives. No one
was getting a tan on this
cruise. We played gin rummy.
We sure could have used
some air freshener in the hold.

A NEW BEGINNING

Evangeline told stories around the campfire,
but she was part wolf and no one believed her:
"Thousands of Recreational Vehicles
plunged from that very cliff in the summer of '91.
A white buffalo by the name of Big Medicine
presided over the clean-up. He celebrated
his thirtieth birthday by sitting perfectly still
in one of the surviving lawn chairs.
And a Great Blue Heron lay unconscious
atop the silvery mountains of kitchenware."
Evangeline was muttering to herself,
her own private legends spilled
like ruptured rosary beads into the flames
while Rory and John prepared the meal
which appeared wavy and frizzled.
Their insecurities were showing, and finally
Frank said, "Frankly, I don't think either of you
are great violinists." It was a poor way
to be speaking, especially as we were
a lost party, or at least a misplaced cluster.
We could hear Evangeline typing something
under a stand of pine. "A trashy romance,"
she called it, and we said, "No, it is a true account,"
but the wolf in her would not let go of that phrase,
and we had to train our sights on her
as commonplace as some endangered species can seem.
Collecting stamps had always given Rory
tremendous gratification, and now he was

pasting a new set into his album sleepily.
Frank was gnashing his teeth as he always did
before a big storm, and John was humming an old tune
left over from his days as a clown in the rodeo.
We were hoping to make New York City
within a couple of days. Evangeline
had contacts in the manicuring business,
and we would pull together and settle our differences.
"After all, it's still America," we said in unison
before blowing out the stars and drifting off
into a deep and unsettling sleep.

THE DOCUMENTARY
WE WERE MAKING

The children ate battered fish wedges
and then started to swim around
a kind of island which turned out to be
the Dowager Empress of China.
Several of them were spitting-up
and turned pale and soon faded from view
rendering the study incomplete and fathomless.
No one was even allowed to speak their names
for more than a thousand years.
And then one fine morning the Dowager herself,
sipping tea, recalled those cockamamie days,
and it made her smile to see those battered
fish wedges again, barely able to swim,
and yet surprisingly fit and handsome.
They were ready to talk about what history
had misunderstood, how some of those
little folk had turned out much better
than anyone could have expected, establishing
the Dixon Ticonderoga pencil factory
in 1388 or some such year, and going on
to become deans of industry and raising
enormous families in the remote Pacific wilderness.
A pencil wrote all this down on its own.
It followed her everywhere for days and

it never stopped taking notes.
One day when she was very old
she walked to the edge of her balcony
and bit the head off of a passing butterfly.
A lost tribe woke under a picnic table,
indicating that a sequel was still possible.

A GLOWWORM, A LEMUR, AND
SOME WOMEN

A glowworm drove by
on its way to a Philosophy Department meeting.
It was in a very large car
and the radio was playing loudly.
Two nude women were praying at the stoplight.
A lemur hopped onto the hood
and asked directions to the nearest gorse bush.
It wore a bonnet, yellow with white lace,
which was quite a surprise to Mr. Donnegal, the driver.
He was already late for the meeting to end all meetings.
He had eaten a sugar donut and was dizzy
with too many ideas about the future of his company
which was a small, donutlike affair.
Everybody who was anybody seemed to be going to a meeting,
the glowworm, who was a solipsist, the lemur
who was not. The two nude women
decided to get dressed and drink some herbal tea,
actually it was ginseng; they were both
homeopathic fiends and not doing very well.
They were very far from deserving this.
It would be hard to find two nicer people anywhere.
Mr. Donnegal checked his watch. He was a frequent
flier, but still he didn't know what was going to happen
next. He stopped to ask directions but there were none.
The lemur was waking after a little nap.
It offered to lead the way. All it wanted was a fair shake,

or a chocolate shake. It was getting late.
Two women, who looked exactly like the other two women,
started to undress in a gazebo which wasn't exactly a gazebo.
Then they realized that they were already undressed
and started to dress very quickly. They were going camping
and decided they would need more and more clothing.
Mr. Donnegal stared at them in disbelief.
They were almost doelike, but with huge, flowery hats,
very much in the fashion of the day, and so he began to sing
and smoke and dwindle, meeting his fate, which was to be late.
The glowworm thought the lemur was an elf child.
Two women—and I'm not sure which two—carried trays
right up to Mr. Donnegal's window, and offered him
a piece of pumpkin chiffon pie. He was beside himself;
in fact, he thought he was having an out-of-the-body experience.
He was gazing through the enlarged eyes of a lemur,
which meant he was, basically, stuck in Madagascar,
and would be terribly late to his meeting.
The glowworm tried to philosophize, he wanted an overview,
he wanted to see something else, like a ballfield
the size of a postage stamp, with the fans asleep at last,
and the hotdogs cooing, paradigmatically, in their buns.

I GOT BLINDSIDED

Sometimes she calls me Chance
and sometimes she calls me Desire.
I was coming out of the laundromat
wearing my little Graceland hat.
What most astounded me on this particular day
was the day itself, my being alive
against such confusion, my being erect,
one could almost say, as opposed
to crawling all around the place
snakeless, beingless, with no face.
Bob Dylan was coming to our tiny town,
a big man, having survived so much,
and having written it down, and
put it to music, why did he bother?
About anything? Especially us.
It was just his way of doing things.
So much the better. And why not us?
Of all people? I was the one
who got drunk, out of necessity.
I missed out on the dinner party,
maybe I was some place else.
She said: "Diminishment of the fauna
has me concerned." I said: "What?"
All this dinner party stuff had me
. . . what is the word . . . perforated?
Perpendicular. I'm perjuring myself
because I want to, because of an ever-
lasting joy. This is what I call

getting things done, well, sort of.
I have never been to a concert.
What would he say? So now, at last,
you are growing up, into a thing thing.
We can expect you to do better soon.
Your sad times are reason for celebration.
Misfit fits right in, like a beautiful stem
of something with no flower, no power,
just a reaching upward with no end.
But Bob Dylan is coming to our town,
and we are subcutaneously prepared,
that is, our fingernails are on edge.

THE NEW CHINESE FICTION

Although the depiction of living forms
was not explicitly forbidden, the only good news
about famines was that the station was empty.
It was about 2 A.M. The truck drove away.
A tropical insect that lives in enormous cities
stroked my hair awkwardly, organizing everyone's
schedule. She drove me back to my hotel
in a misty and allusive style, while the old
schools continued the process of devolution.
Part of the roof was loose and flapped noisily
in the wind, who needed work like that?
Poor brethren, do you have any good prose yet?
The New Chinese fiction is getting better,
I suspect, people walking and thinking and fussing,
with a nest to fly out of, with a less intimate footing.
Are we responsible for their playtimes?
Keep up your music, my dears; there were a lot of people
like that, with strange eyes, green fields and orchards.
The little house they sat in produced simple people,
cars full of blood, all they needed was a hat,
extramusical sounds, purging the emotions.
Expect no mercy, I said, from the sickbay.
And try to imagine Howard Hughes piloting the plane
that flew Cary Grant and Barbara Hutton off

toward their marriage in 1950. Well, don't bother.
The New Chinese fiction shouldn't concern itself
with anything other than a stolen turnip
and a coldness in the heart, and a lit window,
a young man on a horse appearing and then disappearing.

ABANDONED CONCEPTIONS

A leaf stirred on the aspen.
A chunk of earth worked its way free of the hill.
Then it was relatively quiet for a moment.
A grackle said the word
and a young nun broke her rosary,
and a cowboy fell off his barstool.
Then a hush came over the land
and you could hear a ladybug sigh.
My sister fell in love with a dog, and that,
to everyone's surprise, worked out quite nicely.
Oh, I mean, people were hungry and therefore mad.
My father invested wisely and lost his shirt.
My mother went to heaven and came back disappointed.
But since then there's been a mute hand holding us in place.
A kind of satiny, sphinxian unutterableness
has leveled our little forest of thoughts and impressions.
And then a nomad stopped to ask directions,
and we were amazed to be able to assist him.
We all pitched in and made him a cup of coffee
and he started to dance,
and it was clear to us
he was someone else
going nowhere for a long, long time.

WE GO TO A FIRE

Great blasts of hot air are pouring through broken windows
out into the night, a whistling contest for devils.
A powerful smoke ejector rolls up. Its huge, thick hose
looks like a giant caterpillar as it reaches into the warehouse
to suck out the smoke which is blinding the firemen.
Wearily, the firemen drive back to the station house and sleep.
"I suppose they dream of knot tying and gas masks
and tumbler locks, but what do I know?" I said, feeling
a chill come on. We walked on down the street to the café
and sat there contemplating. When, at the next table,
a young girl strikes a match, we dive for cover.
She's reading *The Sorrows of Young Werther* and ignores us.
Rolf claims he is in love and crawls around under the table
for a better look, and in this way we are preserved
from stultification. We are much impressed with the disharmony
of things, and, likewise, the occasional harmony,
such as when a fire chief gives orders to his men.
The serious problems of life, however, are never solved,
and, later, when Rolf asked for her hand in marriage,
she reported us to the authorities, and our flight plan
was ultracontemporary in no particular fashion.
"She's dark but her children will be blond," Rolf whispered.
And as I looked back at her, she began to darkle,
a rare, almost imperceptible, darkishness began
to tease her little fingers as we entered a murky cave
and bade farewell to the darling of this café society,
daughter of the dawn patrol, moccasin flower of radio-
luminescence, because nobody seems to worship her but ourselves.

DESIRE

Crayons could melt upon us for all I care.
I suppress the desire for anything—but my baby!
Diamond doves, keep watch over us.
We're going to lie awake all night
and she might call me "Lieutenant Sterling."
Only a thin wall of corrupt manners
stands between us and a delightful innocence.
Philosophical nights, we'll talk about pineapples:

He: "With miles of pineapples ready to be harvested
there is really little perfume unless
one happens to be bruised or injured."

She: "I can't believe you just said that.
What an unspeakable toad you are."

And that was the last time
I said the word *pineapple,*
though I find myself thinking it
almost constantly.

She doesn't respect me nearly enough,
she could never love me
in the way I deserve to be loved.
So I talk to myself, precisely
in the way I will not tolerate,

which offends me to no end,
and I abhor beyond understanding,
which is at least part of the reason
I desire her still.

WHERE WERE YOU?

The poem has passed.
It was here, in this room,
several hours ago.
Its sleeve brushed my cheek,
and I hesitated, then turned back
to some domestic chore.
I was peeling an onion.
I peeled right down to its core,
then walked away.
My lover stood there
with tears streaming,
and I walked past her.
I stood at the window a long time.
An orange bird with a black beard
looked through me without interest.
Then someone spoke my name
and I ran through all the rooms
desperate for an explanation,
but no one, nothing stirred.
I picked up a blouse
from the back of a chair
and held it up to the light.
I waited several seconds
for its secret meaning
to shine through to me, a pale green.
I felt I was looking up from under water.
A parrot fish swam by.
I held my breath and let go.

Something, someone, was trying to find me,
an assassin, my twin or redeemer,
who would keep me awake nights on end
with his labyrinthine, lachrymose tales
of triumphs and defeats, the narrow
mountain passes and the women who waited,
and the children who disappeared without a trace.
And then the benighted mumbling,
the sighs and barely audible slivers of song.
A shawl covered our knees
and we rocked back and forth
as if some raggedy sense had snuck back into our lives.

PORCH THEORY

Lots of wicker and baskets, a Victorian
birdcage, on rainy nights children sleeping
but not really sleeping under quilts
telling ghost stories. The porch sags.
The children grow into surprising adults.
There's a dinner party, an uncle falls asleep.
The cushions on the wicker couch need mending.
The willow itself is finally dying, having
strangled everything within its great reach
for half-a-century. "Look at those clouds,"
someone says. "The face of God is in there,
somewhere." A cat watches a cricket caught
in a cobweb. Drinks are served. More children
climb on the wicker couch, and grandmother
stares at the croquet set
in the corner, remembering the parrot
her grandfather brought back from the Pacific.

FROM AN ISLAND

Fogged in all day, the long, low horns announcing
the passing of another ghostship.
But we see nothing. It's as if a curtain had been dropped.
Go back into yourself, it says. None of this matters
to you anymore. All that drama, color, movement—
you can live without it. It was an illusion,
a tease, a lie. There is nothing out here but smoke
from the rubble that was everything,
everything you wanted, everything you thought
you needed. Ships passing, forget it.
Children bathing, there's no such thing.
Let go, your island is a mote of dust.
But the horns of the ghostship say, remember us,
we remember you.

THE PARADE AND
AFTER THE PARADE

The parade was a sad little affair,
three or four tiny witches, a pirate,
a Dalmatian, a black cat, a pair of dice.
There was not even a band or a baton.
A single police car led and the rest of us
community-minded cream puffs maundered around
hoping the spirit would strike us.
A cockroach was talking to a hula-goddess
and nibbling on her lace bodice.
It was a dark day downtown
as we drifted off in space.
And then we returned to our houses
and sat down and cried into our hands,
something about not having had a mother
or a father, and this didn't make us
a freak of nature or anything, and I
patted you on the head and we stared
out the window at the oncoming unnecessary risks,
an activity we liked very much.
It was like walking at night with a baby
or falling asleep on a donkey
and spitting off a cliff. Otherwise,
we have pretty much forsaken popular hobbies,
such as wearing camouflage in a forest of stray thoughts.

AN ELAND, IN RETIREMENT

Once the eland was very common,
and traveled in large herds
over the plains of Africa.
But the eland was not a very fast runner,
and it could not defend itself
or get away from its enemies.
Now there is only one, and it lives
in Teaneck, New Jersey—pop., 37,825—
and watches television from
early morning until late at night.
It likes Pop Tarts and little else.
Memories of Africa: it was shaped
like a pear, a few men in turbans
and long flowing robes, wandering
giants with very fancy hair styles
beating drums, and women with
dinner plates in their lips.
Did you know that Mamie Eisenhower's
engagement ring was an exact duplicate
of Dwight's West Point ring, specially
made to fit her hand? Tidbits
such as that have made all of
my aggravation endurable. They were married
on July 1, 1916, in Denver, Colorado.
Mamie's full maiden name was Mary
Geneva Doud and she was born in Boone, Iowa,

on November 14, 1896. Is Mamie still alive?
It seems as if she is. She seldom hunted, I'm told.
Mami, Mami, Mami, we hardly knew ya'.
The less said about "Bess" Truman—
née Elizabeth Virginia Wallace—the better.
I'd rather talk about the salubrious effects
of a bite by a tsetse fly, or the kindness
of cheetahs. Harry called her "the Boss,"
but Harry loved all of his women,
even Margaret. Like an earthworm,
she had a soft body, and like an earthworm
she had no eyes or ears or arms or legs.
I'm just saying that because I am the last
eland and nobody cares, at least nobody in Teaneck.
Margaret Truman was born in 1924.
She played the tuba (I'm joking) and was not very good.
Since moving to America, I have become
very interested in sculpture, and I am particularly
fond of the works of Augustus Saint-Gaudens.
He died in 1907, and his estate in Cornish, N.H.,
has been made a memorial to him, with plaster
and bronze replicas of his work.
His memorial to Clover Adams, Henry Adams'
strange and difficult wife, has puzzled generations.
Clover's suicide and Henry's benign acceptance
is still a cloud to behold in wonder.
Which reminds me: egg noodles of the best grade,
made of fresh eggs and selected wheat flour,

are highly nutritious and are easily digested
even by delicate stomachs, and they are frequently
recommended for invalids and convalescents.
Lobsters afford more phosphorus than any other food.
They are, perhaps unconsciously, on this account
much eaten by the nerve-racked workers of the great cities.
As you can see, I have taken it upon myself
to keep abreast of the times, as unlikely as it is
that I will have an opportunity to pass on this information
to any successor. I have, for the record, agreed
to three "dates" since the last of my kind passed on:
the first was with an impala; it had a very attractive
purple-black blaze on its forehead, and moved
with great grace, but finally it was too jumpy.
It would jump ten feet over nothing, and this seemed to me
entirely unnecessary and unnerving. The second
was a disaster: a wildebeest by the name of Norman.
Norman would run around in circles snorting,
tossing his head as if it were on fire.
This was not my idea of a good time.
My last attempt at finding a mate is better left untold.
A bat-eared fox. I was desperate, and temporarily
lost all sense of decorum, for which I am truly chagrined.
He was cute, a fine pet, perhaps, but hardly
a suitable father for my progeny.
A red sleeve, that's all I know, a red sleeve
reaches through me. I can dress wounds,
endure night duty, but I have never been

to the cinema. In fact, by now I am old and cranky
and it's all that I can do to change the channel
and watch these little people solve their crimes,
so dear to their hearts. They are all selling
sanitation products on the side, or mainly.
Why was I spared, I'll never know.
In the vast savanna scrub
a melancholy bug preens its antennae
in the glow of the worn-out sun.
Bureaucratic gossip, don't take any notice of it.

JIM LEFT THE PET CEMETERY
WITH A FEELING OF DISGUST

We hope to avoid everlasting mistakes.
We had a custom-made coffin for the boa.
It was fifty times longer than a pencil box.
As for the parakeet, she fit inside a snowball.
Music played, *Jim's Total Health Book* was read.
"Mind your eggs," was all it said.
Jim walked around the snowfield and photographed eggs.
We installed a birdfeeder over the gravestone.
The deceased seemed pleased.
A woman no one knew tried to buy socks from everybody.
She said, "This is a town made out of nothing,"
and no one disagreed. Dagwood drew faces on the eggs.
"It's just that we aren't on the map yet," I replied.
Old Long Plain Road, who wants to admit to that?
The one who chiseled the stone took pride in his work.
The trees, after sixty long winters, had never looked better.
Despite the departure of our dear friends
the weather was on the mend, prospects
improved with the passing of each hour.
It's strange how we survive, the few
of us who do from time to time: the others
thought so too. They relied on us
to complete a mission, which was futile
but down to the basics—a new frying pan,
a red broom, why do they always insist

on the garish in a time of gloom?
Jim walked down to the river and looked like a reed.
I mean, he looked at a reed, and sighed
in a melancholic way. There was a trading post
on the other shore and there was no practical way
to get there. A boy named Ashley walked out of the clouds.
He was named after a town in central Pennsylvania.
"I didn't mean to," he said, and Jim sat down and cried.
Some time passed in a large, irregular way.
Dagwood had his name changed to "Bill."
And this was a good thing for everyone, everyone
took turns patting him on his head,
which eventually weakened him and lowered him
into the sand. It was a yeoman on a passing tugboat
who finally sang, "So long, Bill, it's been good to know ya'."
That little bit of good timing provided the rest
with the motivation to revamp the tattered ends
of their ceremonies, less pomp, and no circumstance
would haunt, henceforth, their seemingly interminable days.

THE NEW WORK

The great cat was dreaming of me,
but each time it tried
it fell just short of imagining the vastness of my nights.
So it said, let's start with a little thing,
like his socks, and then, with some luck, we'll build from there.
His socks, with great celestial storms woven around them,
are slipping as he strides across
the ancient war-torn cities whistling an unknown anthem.
(This is very promising: I can see he is a noble figure
out of his mind with grief—the very stuff of poetry!)
When a small dog dashes from an alley and nips at his ankles
he appears dazed and confused—who'd have thought
he was so fragile, all that wisdom and courage
so easily dispersed. He peers around through the crowd
as if searching for some familiar reference point.
The dog licks his hands and he appears sheepishly grateful.
The whole scene has passed unremarked upon by the passersby,
who, in contrast now, seem to be charged with splendid missions:
the maid with her baguette hoists her banner straight into the
        slaughter;
the unshaven worker in his grimy overalls rescues her from oblivion
by doffing his cap and bowing slightly.
An officer from a nearby bank is stirring a single cube of sugar
into his demitasse: he knows that worker,
and takes a modicum of satisfaction in recalling
the loan he refused to grant him the Christmas before last.
But that is neither here nor there. The sun is breaking through the
        clouds

for the first time in more than a week.
The great cat has turned its eye elsewhere,
and while at first I was flattered to think that my poor self
could be elevated by such attention I readily confess to the doubt
the whole project filled me with, though doubt itself does seem
    deserving
of an immense meditation, ending, no doubt, with all those fine
    details
we can't seem to escape—the perfume clinging to a paper clip,
the hedge clippers in the bathtub.
The great cat is pacing the floor
(I can't see him but I sense him everywhere).
He wants to start over, he wants most of all to edit me out.
His new work begins: "The simoom is a strong, dry wind
that spreads mayonnaise over the deserts of North Africa."

WE LOVE THE VENERABLE HOUSE

Full of dictionaries and photographs,
photographs of dictionaries and photographs
of photographs. A house astir with music
and almanacs, noodles, soups, spoons, candlesticks.
A house skylarking with broken eyeglasses and books,
pillows and postcards, notebooks and old letters,
amused by pencils, brooms, paintings and puppets,
interrogating lead soldiers and real war medals.
A house contemplating typewriters leaning against walls,
shocked at magazines spilling out of shelves,
sleepy house of windowfans and staplers,
maps and buttons and flashlights, seashells,
magnifying glasses, stamps, bones, shaving brushes
and arrowheads, lighters, matches, masks,
pocketwatches, thread, gourds.
Dizzy house of telescopes, tin boxes, foreign coins, ticket stubs.
Lucky house of lightbulbs, programs, shoes,
balls of string, spools of wire, tacks,
statues, models, receipts.
It's a long journey, they always say.
There's always something to forget or laugh about.
A bird walks an imaginary dog across the lawn and shouts,
"Heel, Brownie!" every few minutes.

IN MY OWN BACKYARD

I've seen fox, deer, wild turkey, pheasant, skunk,
snakes, moles, guinea hens. I've thrown a boomerang
that never came back.

I've played croquet, badminton, wiffle ball, frisbee.
My flower garden has never amounted to much, but there it is,
black-eyed Susans and tiger lilies pushing up
against the odds.

There's an old weathered chicken coop full
of empty paint cans, a homemade wooden wheelbarrel.

Beyond that is an ersatz compost heap—I'm not consciously
composting anything.

A mulberry tree, a red maple, a spirea bush.

My neighbor hits a golf ball into my yard once in a while.
I watch him from the kitchen window.
I share a laundry line with him and his wife.
We catch up on neighborhood news about once a year:
he died, she left him, they took a trip to Canada.

Sometimes I walk the property line, first the side
adjacent to the forest, past the birch trees
and disused doghouse, then along the vacant field
where local kids played softball forty years ago—
the pitcher's rubber is still in place.

I try to appear as if I am inspecting something in the grass,
but I am a little daft, touched, as they say,
a little on my way out to pasture.

I grab my throat and wrestle me to the ground.
"There, there," I say, "lighten up ol' boy."
"It's a free country, it's your own backyard."
I listen intently: sky and daisies burlesque each other,

bivouacked between worlds.

THE MORNING NEWS

Satellites document a shift
in an ant colony. A spy joins
a circus—a clown leaps from
a bridge. A prima ballerina
loses consciousness after sharing
a recreational drug called Ecstasy
with a steeplejack. Both dream
of snakes but the snakes swallow
each other and there is not a trace
of all this. I am in my bath,
it's a Monday, I am almost asleep
listening to the news—a mudslide
has erased a small country.
The world, that mudslide, was
moving away from me. I felt
as if I were on one of those
level airport escalators, too late
to walk. And the world was
incredibly beautiful (w/o me).
An afterthought to my dream,
my dream of swans, six or seven
of them, about to slide over
an immense waterfall. I have won
a trip to Hawaii for two.
Was she a Sister of Mercy, or
A Sister of the Damned?
All the shoppers in aisle three
are sexually starved simultaneously.

All but one prefers a speeded-up
life, a life that can be discounted
with the presentation of coupons.
So early in the morning and already
a child has left home and fallen asleep
on her pink valise beneath a tulip tree.

SUMMER, MAINE COAST

A boy fishing,
what does he want?
He reels in seaweed all day,
his mother in a folding chair in back of him
turning the pages of a romance novel.
A boat speeds by.
A sunset begins to melt.
No one knows where they came from,
where they are going.
But for now, it is enough,
to cast into the lapping, silver waters,
the seaweed this time leaps and pulls,
indeed, it even dreams it is a bluefish,
and to turn the page
to discover our knight in shining armor
was really a two-bit cad.
This was a day they would both remember,
a day of low-flying cormorants,
a cool breeze in summer,
and the red and white ferries hauling
the island people back to their defenses.
Later, the boy and his mother
walked along the rocky shore
and were never seen again.

COLOR IN THE GARDEN

It is important to forget, if possible.
And to advance as a pioneer.
For in this realm each pioneer is certainly
doing no harm in the hope of greatly
enriching—the garden? Possibly.
But himself beyond doubt.
One may give free reign to imagination,
no end or beginning in the sequence:
indigo, indigo, violet, red, red, red.
There is a growing affinity
until all others are attenuated, dead.
If these are set like wedges in a circle,
the same guiding principle
is carried a little further, and put to bed.
Like a plague of oranges in a green submarine.
For now it appears that each color
leads to the next inevitably.
A theory popularized by some
could not be a greater fallacy.
Consequently, white flowers divide,
never reconcile. The garden is so strong
that reconciliation feels necessary.
It can be explained *in no other way*.
Thence to violet-blue and at last pure blue.
The eye observes, look where it will,
color. Long before the form of an object
is noted or recognized, the last lingering
mental vision is its color. Sick people

are affected, workers, animals and insects.
Butterflies love mauves and lavenders.
Bees make savage onslaughts against anyone
rash enough to wear red. The housefly prefers
white. Red life itself will not be denied.
For the weak and ailing to sit among,
for rapidly growing children to sit in the midst
of, for the aged and feeble to dwell with.
We gather that it is an unfavorable color.
Not until they were removed from it
or allowed to spend some time in the "blue" room
did they become normal. A blue garden
for the highly strung, for the tired
businessman, for the child
given to violent outbursts.
If the temperament is sluggish,
keep it out of the garden.
Men whose lives are spent in rose breeding
use yellow to delineate the halo shining
from the head of a saint or a martyr.
If well-handled, it may yield
unusual and ethereal beauty.
It seems like a stain they have left there,
which probably does not exist—never did
and never will. So there is departure,
even if slight, from flawlessness.
Yet withstanding this, the dazzling quality remains.
A wraithlike shimmering, ghostly beauty

haunts the memory; it is not often seen.
Under moonlight, the senses are bewitched,
a deep sea of fleecy clouds, over whose rim
the water spills continually like a veil.

INSPIRATION

The two men sat roasting in their blue suits
on the edge of a mustard field.
Lucien Cardin, a local painter,
had suggested a portrait.
President and Vice President of the bank branch,
maybe it would hang in the lobby
inspiring confidence. It might even
cast a little grace and dignity
on the citizens of their hamlet.
They were serious men with sober thoughts
about an unstable world.
The elder, Gilbert, smoked his pipe
and gazed through his wire-rims beyond the painter.
The sky was eggshell blue,
and Lucien knew what he was doing
when he begged their pardon
and went to fetch the two straw hats.
They were farmers' hats, for working in the sun.
Gilbert and Tom agreed to wear them
to staunch their perspiration,
but they knew too the incongruity
their appearance now suggested.
And, as for the lobby of their bank,
solidarity with the farmers, their customers.
The world might go to war—Louis flattened
Schmeling the night before—but a portrait
was painted that day in a field of mustard

outside of Alexandria, Ontario,
of two men, even-tempered and levelheaded,
and of what they did next there is no record.

WORSHIPFUL COMPANY OF
FLETCHERS

I visited the little boy
at the edge of the woods.
It's still not clear to me
where he really lives.
He'd live with animals
if they'd take him in,
and there would never be
a need to speak. "Who knows,
when you grow up you may be
President," I said, trying
to break the spell.
He flinched as though struck.
"Perhaps something in the field
of numismatics," I continued,
"would be less stressful.
A correspondence school course.
No need to leave the home,
no wretched professor thwacking
your knuckles. In no time
you could hang out your shingle—
STAMPS AND COINS. No more than
one customer per week,
I feel fairly certain: some nerd
who can barely talk—
I'm certainly not speaking of
yourself here—browsing

the liberty dimes and Indian head
pennies, if you see what I mean."
I had meant to comfort him,
but the feral child was now
mewling, and this annoyed me.
"I doubt you have what it takes—
discipline, fastidiousness,
honesty, devotion—to serve
as a manservant, a butler,
to a gentleman of rank and
high-calling. No, I'm afraid
no amount of training
could instill those virtues
into one such as you."
I paused to let the acid burn.
The doe-eyed lad wiped his nose
on his tee-shirt and peeked over
his shoulder into the woods
which seemed to beckon him.
A breeze rustled the leaves
above our heads, and the boy swayed.
A pileated woodpecker tapped
some Morse code into a dead oak tree.
At last, the boy said, "You regret
everything, I bet. You came here
with a crude notion of righting

all that was wrong with your own
bitter childhood, but you have become
your own father—cruel, taunting—
who had become his father, and so on.
It's such a common story.
I wish I could say to you:
'You'd make a fine shepherd,'
but you wouldn't. Your tireless needs
would consume you the first night."
And, with that, the boy stepped forward
and kissed me on the cheek.

HAPPY AS THE DAY IS LONG

I take the long walk up the staircase to my secret room.
Today's big news: they found Amelia Earhart's shoe, size 9.
1992: Charlie Christian is bebopping at Minton's in 1941.
Today, the Presidential primaries have failed us once again.
We'll look for our excitement elsewhere, in the last snow
that is falling, in tomorrow's Gospel Concert in Springfield.
It's a good day to be a cat and just sleep.
Or to read the *Confessions* of Saint Augustine.
Jesus called the sons of Zebedee the Sons of Thunder.
In my secret room, plans are hatched: we'll explore the Smoky
       Mountains.
Then we'll walk along a beach: Hallelujah!
(A letter was just delivered by Overnight Express—
it contained nothing of importance, I slept through it.)
(I guess I'm trying to be "above the fray.")
The Russians, I know, have developed a language called "Lincos"
designed for communicating with the inhabitants of other worlds.
That's been a waste of time, not even a postcard.
But then again, there are tree-climbing fish, called anabases.
They climb the trees out of stupidity, or so it is said.
Who am I to judge? I want to break out of here.
A bee is not strong in geometry: it cannot tell
a square from a triangle or a circle.
The locker room of my skull is full of panting egrets.
I'm saying that strictly for effect.
In time I will heal, I know this, or I believe this.
The contents and furnishings of my secret room will be labelled

and organized so thoroughly it will be a little frightening.
What I thought was infinite will turn out to be just a couple
of odds and ends, a tiny miscellany, miniature stuff, fragments
of novelties, of no great moment. But it will also be enough,
maybe even more than enough, to suggest an immense ritual and
    tradition.
And this makes me very happy.

ABOUT THE AUTHOR

James Tate's *Selected Poems* was published in 1991, for which he received the Pulitzer Prize and the William Carlos Williams Award. He teaches at the University of Massachusetts in Amherst.